BLACK SHEEP

DON'T ASK STUPID QUESTIONS

Black Sheep

To My Mother
Though you were taken far too soon, the quality of your light
remains to guild my feet and inform my soul.

To those who have stood by my side in spite of my flaws, and
because of them.

It Ain't What You Don't Know That Gets You Into Trouble. It's What You Know for Sure That Just Ain't So.

Attributed to Mark Twain

Contents

Preface

The more we recognize what we are doing and why, the less power that fear has over us. As we become more comfortable, this confidence becomes second nature. I was not born with confidence, I am an introvert. As a child, I was shy, too scared to go into a store on my own. I've always been very self-conscious, and I have insecurities like everyone else.

When people say they can't do what I do because they aren't like me, I should find a simpler way to show it. Just because I see how simple and easy the change is, others may not.

One of the reasons I started this was acknowledging that no matter how much you care for someone and want to help them grow and achieve their goals, it's another human being with thoughts and feelings of their own. If I am getting frustrated, then I need to look at myself. At some point, I need to ask honest questions about what role I am playing in creating this problem.

If I make content like this, then hopefully people that want it will work through it and use what works for them. At the same time, be accepting of people's right to choose, and celebrate our differences.

I am not afraid to be vulnerable like this simply because if I show that I am human, then you will be less likely to think I'm special or more talented than you are. My path led me to ask these questions, your path has led you across this perspective here and now.

I saw these qualities in others, and I got curious. I spoke to people, read books, and observed and tested on myself and others. I didn't think about writing a book, it just happened naturally.

I wanted to give someone a list of questions I would ask as a training aid. After about ten questions I asked myself, how would it be received and understood? If I was just starting out and I read this list of questions, having none of my years of learning, would I understand how to ask questions going forward? Honestly no. I had put together a list of questions I would ask as part of a larger strategy of calm information gathering.

If the training was going to be useful, then understanding the 'why' is important. I needed to dive into why people aren't willing to ask questions. Fear and insecurity.

I have my own fears about publishing this first book. The learning curve has been steep in this process. The feedback will no doubt be a tough teacher too. All the lessons will shape the next one which is already in progress.

This is a structured and hopefully relatable attempt, to share something in a way that will bear fruit. Practically and simply.

1

SPOT THE STUPID QUESTION

There is no such thing as a stupid question. How many times have you heard that phrase used to make everyone feel safe? How about these? The only stupid question is the one you don't ask. I want to encourage you to be involved, ask me anything, there are no stupid questions. If you have a question please ask it, the chances are someone else has the same question and is too scared to ask.

Imagine you were on a game show, and I said, 'This is your final question, it is for 1 million dollars. Get it right and you're a millionaire. Get it right and you're flying home in first class. However, get it wrong and you're going home in cattle class with sweet nothing. Your question for 1 million dollars is, True or false? There is no such thing as a stupid question.' I'm guessing you thought the answer was obvious until you have a lot to lose. Would you be finding ways to justify it as true? Or would you be trying to think of examples of stupid ones to prove it false? It's false and I'll prove it.

Imagine you are the captain of a sailboat (sounds cooler than cargo ship). You are in the harbor and cargo is being loaded onto your boat. You have no stops along the way. The cargo is very urgent. A lot of people are losing money while they wait for you, so you are in a hurry to get there. You take pride in your work and put a lot of effort into what you do. The cargo will be there as fast as possible because you know how important it is.

It doesn't matter whether you have sailed before, just imagine you are on the deck of the boat. It's a sailboat so the perfect situation for us would be to have a good wind blowing. Without wind, I'm sure you'll agree that you won't be sailing anywhere in a hurry.

Everyone is relying on you and losing money while they wait. If you have consistent wind, it's a 5-day trip. Everyone on land believes it should take 5-days from door to door. The cargo still needs to be loaded and unloaded, so the best case is 7 days for this delivery. The deadline is a little unreasonable, but you will do everything in your power to make it happen as always.

You're standing on the deck, a warm day as your t-shirt flaps in the stiff breeze. But as you start getting underway, your temperature starts to rise as your t-shirt stops flapping with the drop in wind. Lovely weather for reading on the beach. But you need wind, so it's like a traffic jam when you're already late... (That's catchy, someone should use it in a song or something)

When the wind picks up, so do your spirits. It's easier for you and the crew if there's wind because you don't have to keep making changes to the boat. You are using all your skills to find as much

2

wind and speed as possible but it's inconsistent. After all, it's the wind, not electricity, you can't turn it on and off when you want to.

With all your effort and dedication, you arrive at port after 8 days. You've done your best, and you're proud of your crew. You are tired, frustrated, and late for your return trip. The office had already scheduled it to start on day 6. They need the goods you are bringing back very urgently; people are losing money while they wait for you, so you are in a hurry to get back there.

For those on land dealing with customers and managers, the pressure is constant. Customers are demanding their goods and they are unhappy about the delays. The bosses are telling them to sell more and keep the customer happy. They complain about how long you are taking whenever anyone asks why the goods are late. And every delivery is late.

Because expectations aren't being met on most days, people are getting irritated. A manager is tired of deliveries being late all the time and he decides he has had enough. 'I'm going to sort this out and give that captain a piece of my mind because this is unacceptable. I don't care what the excuse is, that boat will start arriving on time or we will look for someone who can.'

The manager calls you in. You notice he is a little red in the face, maybe the breathing seems a little heavier, there's an edge in his voice, and he doesn't greet you. You are tired, stressed, and don't have time to spare for a meeting with cargo to deliver. 'Why are you always late?' he growls. 'We are going as fast as we can. We are working around the clock.' you say. 'Rubbish,

3

you guys are taking chances and I'm telling you right now to stop stuffing around!'

Most interactions will end right there, with one person walking away. The manager will hear no more and just wants results, and the subordinate, hating his unreasonable, ungrateful boss and wishing he could leave.

Sometimes you are a little tougher and willing to stand your ground. You say, 'How can you say we are wasting time, we can't get there any faster, it's impossible. If you buy us an engine we could go faster.' Imagine it, he already believes you aren't working, now you are asking for an engine. Now he doesn't just think you are lazy, but arrogant too. You want an engine so you can do even less work and just drink rum all day. His eyes are bulging, 'I'm tired of your excuses! If you don't get your act together, I'll get someone who can, now get back to work and stop wasting time!'

You complain to your team and family about this ungrateful company and how stupid they are. 'Those pencil pushers don't have a clue what they are doing. If they put an engine on the boat, we could maintain speed when the wind dies. They don't see that if we get an engine, we can do more trips and make more money.' Venting to your friend sounds something like, 'What the hell do they expect me to do, I can't control the wind?' and, 'They think we are stupid.' Your friend says, 'Why don't you tell them, maybe they will listen?' You say that you have told them, and they never listen to anything you say. Your friend asks why you don't leave if you aren't happy? You love what you do and it's probably the same everywhere, so there's no point complaining about it.

<u>Spot the stupid question.</u>

The manager believes he already knows the answers. He is convinced that you are lazy, and you'll find excuses. He isn't interested in what you have to say. He probably said as much to the other finger pointers in the office before your meeting.

First you were doing nothing. Now you have the audacity to ask for an engine so that you can be even more useless. If you only did your job, the company would do more trips and make more money. He isn't going to lose more money on fuel, while you do even less work.

Good questions are helpful and make an effort to understand. Stupid questions are hurtful and make the situation worse.

A stupid question is one that only causes a lot of stress. There was no intention to understand why the expectations aren't being met. The question, 'Why are you always late?' was used as an accusation. The purpose was to cast blame. It wastes time because it upsets everyone without being productive. The problem isn't being solved.

<u>Let's make it easy.</u>

No doubt you've seen this play out many times. Both parties believe that they are right, and the other is wrong. Both sides want the other side to change in some way. But they expect to stay the same themselves.

Here is my challenge to you. Find situations where people are blaming each other for things going wrong. It's our opportunity to lead with questions. Let's try to change the situation through understanding. Focusing on solving the problem for everyone. As we progress, we will build on this basic concept of being mindful of people.

Step 1: Ask an actual question. Even if you think you know the answer.

Step 2: Keep your mouth shut and listen. Listening to understand instead of listening to respond.

2

AN UNHEALTHY COMPETITION

I can trace so many life decisions back to a life-changing afternoon when I was 10. We were visiting friends and the Monaco Grand Prix was on TV. I found myself sat there glued to the screen. It was the first time I had seen a motor race and I was hooked. Suddenly there was a direction. Reading car magazines, collecting model cars, and posters for my bedroom walls suddenly became my life.

When I changed schools, I made a friend who was also mad about motors. We became best friends by default because we had the same interests. We needed to prove ourselves to one another constantly. Somehow our relationship was competitive from the start. Neither of us would ever admit to not knowing an answer. Admitting that we didn't know something would be admitting that the other person was superior.

Someone would ask us how something on a car worked. Since we both felt we had to know everything, we always answered with conviction. The thing is, I didn't know very much but I couldn't admit it, so I made up things on the fly. I eventually realized that my friend was just as scared as I was. I know this because he would back my bullshit completely and even add to it himself, but I was just making it up as I went along. I laugh about the comical value of it now, but the truth at the time was stressful and toxic.

We were acting as rivals. Our egos were completely in the way of learning together and helping each other. It was an 'ah ha' moment for me to realize how we wasted our talent and friendship, and how toxic the situation was. We were in school for heaven's sake. We did this every day without being aware of how draining it was.

So, I decided to try something crazy. I decided to be truly honest with my friend. I shared my thoughts, leaving myself completely exposed. He admitted it was true for him too. I suggested we stop pretending and hiding our ignorance from each other, and everyone else. We committed to helping one another and growing as a team. The relief I felt was like thinking you've overslept, before realizing it's the weekend.

As is often the case, in reality, people are resistant to change. My friend chose not to follow through, so I had to make a choice of my own. It was a powerful feeling getting rid of that burden which also allowed me freedom. It made absolutely no sense to go back into that pattern when I had seen it for what it was. I had absolute conviction that this was the right way forward.

It was time to stop hiding and pretending. I wanted to see things as they are and not spend my energy pretending to be perfect. I wanted the freedom to say I don't know and to explore.

After leaving school I still refused to claim I understood things when I didn't. I had to learn that it was safe to speak up and that's the gift I now want to give you. I've become comfortable asking questions. There's just no anxiety about needing to know everything anymore, I'm free.

If someone has explained something and I still don't understand then I say so. Ask them to be patient and try again. The confusion is often caused by the other person assuming I know something that I don't. That's my opportunity to learn from them.

Do I feel stupid asking people to explain things every day? Not at all, people like to be appreciated and valued so everyone wins. I've learned a lot because I've had so many teachers. In turn, people ask me for help because of what I've learned.

The other huge take away is that everyone has a limit to their understanding. That has given me a lot of confidence. No matter how long someone has been doing a job, I have seen that they have gaps in their knowledge just like everyone else.

All over the world people are trying to improve on current ways of doing things every single day. If you have been doing a job for years, the odds are there are new ways to do what you do. If you can accept that statement, then surely you can accept that it is reasonable for you to have room to grow. And that's okay. By the same token can you accept that it is true for everyone around you too?

3

FAILING FORWARD

Losing my cheese

There was no space to sit in the conference hall we used for her memorial. A mass of humanity flooded the space till it spilled over into the hallway of the government building. The same was true at her funeral service. We never understood how many lives she touched in her 49 years.

Like her love, milk and cheese were abundant in our home. It has a sweetness that is soft and delicious. It was important to me without me realizing just how much. It became part of how I understood the world. My mom would buy milk and cheese in bulk to save money. Looking back I can see now that even though we had very little, one of her amazing gifts was to make us forget that. She was a great cook.

She was a single mom supporting three kids on a shoestring budget. I don't think there was ever a time that any of us fought to have a take-out if she didn't suggest it. Why would we? We were eating a different family favorite almost every night. My mom hated that word, I can still hear her saying, 'Who is SHE? SHE is the cat's mother.'

She used food as a powerful form of love and security. With such passion and care for her children she was driven to make a low-cost meal better than anything a restaurant could put up. There was no way she was going to let us feel poor or inferior. Do you think for a moment we would rather be in a rich family?

At the end of my school career, I began to have stomach cramps regularly. Mild at first but it was getting worse. The pain got so bad I had to be taken to hospital. They treated the pain which helped so I did that myself going forward instead of finding the cause.

My girlfriend at the time, possibly feeling neglected by my problematic tummy depriving her of my sparkling personality, or tired of me being a crampy tummy whiny brat, hopefully the first but probably the second if I'm being completely honest with myself, Googles my symptoms. She tells me I'm going to die. No, not really but I felt that a part of me was because Doctor Google was suggesting lactose intolerance.

How would you feel? You've only ever known coffee and tea to have milk, in my case at least half a mug, and you get told to stop immediately. If you already take your coffee black, ask the people you talk to how willing they are to stop taking milk in their coffee. Cooking had started to interest me, but we used milk and delicious salty cheddar in many dishes.

Whenever I went to a restaurant with my girlfriend, I had to find dairy-free options. Everyone told me that they'd never be able to live that way, they would rather suffer. I had felt that way too for a while. But I realized that was stupid quite quickly. Now, I just felt robbed and cheated. I would just order something without dairy and try not to think about it too much. It was just food to survive and not something to enjoy anymore.

I started to notice something strange after a while. At first, I was just relieved that the food I was ordering wasn't horrible. It was different from what I was used to. I was sure it was supposed to be. I didn't want to admit that the new things I was trying were really tasty. I had been refusing to see what was right in front of me. It was getting hard to pretend that all these different foods weren't really good. It took a while for me to give myself permission to enjoy food again.

It was like I had been stuck in a room. Everything I knew, how I believed the world worked, was in that room. I was shoved out the door. Forced out of my comfort zone, and feeling robbed at the same time. But out of that loss, I came to see that there's a much greater number of amazing food in the world that don't rely on dairy. Lactose free dairy is on the rise these days but I'm grateful for that struggle. It gave me far more than it took.

Burning with conviction

People were putting their families in danger. They were trying to save money by changing to gas appliances instead of electrical ones. Even though they used licensed installers like they were supposed to, gas installations were being done in unsafe and illegal ways to save money.

The problem was the safety cage around the cylinders. Some installations needed it to keep kids and animals safe. It would also slow a fire down to give the fire department time to respond. They were just so damn expensive. In many cases, it would be a deal breaker if you insisted that a cage had to be used. Some installers would still give a certificate in those cases because they needed the money.

What if there was a way to make the cage cheaper? That would allow the installer to make money and the customer to save money while doing it safely. The existing cages were large, fixed boxes making them difficult to work with. I designed a flat-pack cage. Parts that were easy to carry, fast to assemble, and cheaper.

To make the cage as cheap as possible I had to work with a factory next door to mine. They would do electro-plating on the cages to stop them from rusting. That was a great way to make a better-quality cage. I didn't need to spend time painting and the factory next door would have much-needed work. Everyone who saw it was impressed and the orders flowed.

I bought as much steel as I could afford believing I had a winner. That's when the universe punched me in the gut. The factory next door suddenly received big orders which was great for them. For the cage business, it was a death sentence.

Every day they told me not to worry, they would make a plan to have some parts plated the next day. That went on for nearly two months. We were supposed to start with 20 cages a week, but we didn't even do 10 in total in those two months. I had no product to sell and I was out of money.

I had terrible feelings of defeat and failure. Why had I believed that I could reinvent cages and make gas installations better and cheaper? I felt sick to my stomach and worthless. On the day that I hit this state of hopelessness and worthlessness, I went home early. Having given up, I made a sandwich. I was going to need to find a job and admit to myself that I was useless while trying to convince someone that I wasn't and give me a job. As you can tell, I was feeling quite sorry for myself.

I relax with my sandwich at the kitchen counter. My mind is numb and blank. A question pops into my mind. How does this plating process work? To be clear, this is a chemical plating process. I failed chemistry at school because I had no interest at all in that subject. Plating is a business on its own and from what I had seen it would take huge amounts of money to start. But I'm sitting there with nothing better to do, so what the hell, let me entertain my curiosity, and take my mind off how totally screwed I am.

I learn that there are all sorts of ways to do plating. Some of them don't need electrical rectifiers (big electrical machine things that cost lots of money) so you could start with less. Suddenly I'm wondering if I've been stuck in that room again. Was I missing the possibilities?

How am I going to do this with very, very little money? I download a textbook and start writing down questions. I find a supplier willing to teach me and help me find a way to make this happen. In the end with the help of some people close to me and my supplier come teacher, I put together a system with so little money it would make your penny-pinching granny proud.

I was back to working from 6 am to 10 pm, sometimes later. But working alone and the process was too complicated to hire unskilled people to help. Because I can't afford skilled people with such an affordable price on the cages, I'm stuck again. I hadn't anticipated how other people might struggle to grasp the dangers of the plating process we were using.

I had just saved the business and now I was staring defeat in the face again. But I had pulled off something big against the odds with just imagination and creativity. What if I could do it again?

Making cages out of sheet metal was an idea that kept coming up, but we weren't allowed to use it, because the law called for a lot of ventilation. No cages that were made with sheet metal were legal because they didn't have enough holes. I found a way to cut enough holes on the cheap but it was still sheet metal.

Customers didn't want to risk getting in trouble. So, I took the cage to the head of the gas safety association and showed him that I wanted to help the industry. He helped me get a meeting with the person responsible for assessing and approving safety devices for the fire department. Getting that endorsement letter was a huge win. It was officially recognized.

It had been an epic struggle, but I had made it. The first orders were placed immediately. The new factory that did the prototyping was fast and enthusiastic. I placed the first big order but they also produced nothing for months. Again, after pulling a bunny out of a hat, the universe had given me a sucker punch.

This is usually the part of the story where something lucky happens. The fairy-tale ending sees thousands of cages being made, the world is a better place, and everyone lives happily ever after. This is not that kind of story. This story ends with me getting a temporary job while I put my life back together. I had run out of time and money, and my personal life collapsed like a chocolate easter bunny in a hot car.

A project that was supposed to last for a few months, turned into a journey lasting more than two years. It was a gift for me. I would be given the freedom to do what I do best, help people. To support them solve problems every day.

You will fail and that's ok but what doors are opening for you? When something seems hopeless and impossible you can try to get back in the box or find a new way. But don't think you have to come up with a plan on your own. Ask everyone for ideas, and make sure to consider the crazy ones. If something hasn't been done you'll cherish that success the most.

4

LET'S TALK ABOUT FEARS

Let's start by saying they are real.
Sure, you've been told there's nothing to be afraid of. Or it's all in the mind and to get over yourself. We won't do that here. Just because other people don't struggle with your fears, doesn't make them any less real for you while you have them.

Let's acknowledge that they are real and shine a light on these insecurities. I hope you will be open to the perspective that I want to share with you now. You may have more power than you think.

Thoughts:
  What if I am wrong and I look stupid?
  What if I was supposed to know the answer and I look stupid?
  I don't want the attention on me.

Physical and emotional:
  Anxiety.

Inadequate and insecure about whether I was good enough.

Concern that people would think I'm stupid, irritating, or annoying.

Talk about self-doubt...

Ok, I admit that I'm human not a natural-born talent. If you're only wanting to hear from someone who is undefeated then that's ok. If this ends up as an audiobook, I hope your wasted credit will be refunded. As for the minutes of your life spent on this, I've got nothing for you but gratitude. If you are still with me here's how I got past some of this personal drama.

When I was scared, I tried to understand why. There are many ways to work through things, but I am going to show you things I noticed about perceptions, assumptions, and fear.

Rise of the ego, and stupid assumptions about stupidity and stupid questions...

Perception - A belief or opinion held by many people and based on how things seem.

Quote, Cambridge dictionary

Assumption – Something that you accept as true without question or proof.

Quote, Cambridge dictionary

As children, we were taught that adults have the answers. We were taught to listen because they said so. Their word was law because we relied on them for everything in our world like food and protecting us from ourselves. It makes sense that at this early age we are associating rank with absolute understanding in all things.

Then we go to school and we add another layer of conditioning. There is mostly only one correct answer and if yours is different, then you are wrong and that's bad. Perfect copy answers are the aim.

I appreciate that this is a system where one person can try to pass on knowledge to large groups of kids in a systematic and timely fashion. The intention is good, and teachers are completely underappreciated. I'm just pointing out a side effect of this approach. Being wrong or different from that mold is discouraged and seen as a problem. The standard copy answer is the measure of your understanding, we label those kids who score well in this system as smart.

As much as I want to show how wrong this is, I'm going to trust that you know some people who don't hold degrees, but outshine people who do. The important point here is that you see how these perceptions and assumptions are being formed as we move through life.

Next comes our work life and another few layers of conditioning. As you grow up you are witnessing a lot of what to expect from life through your parents. When you enter the working world yourself everything mentioned so far gets reinforced and society drives the status agenda. Now it's money, position, authority, respect, bigger car, bigger house, bigger stuff, and more stuff...

You might be thinking that it's just an interesting theory. Ever heard of Maslow's hierarchy of needs. This is a standard psychological description of how people prioritize things that is widely taught in sales and marketing. Imagine a pyramid with five layers. Each layer represents what we are likely to focus on starting from the bottom. First our physical needs like food and shelter. Secondly our safety. Third is to belong or be loved. Fourth is our self-esteem. Fifth is what we aspire to be.

Once our most basic survival needs are met, we start focusing on self-worth. Entering the working world, you aren't just a passive observer of Maslow's hierarchy of needs, you are expected to be a participant.

I'm not making a case against good marketing, but showing some of the factors that create resistance toward asking questions. By all means, have ambition and want more for yourself. The point is to bring your attention to how we are conditioned into certain perceptions. Perceptions, based on nothing more than ideas, not some rule of physics.

With that in mind, how do we measure our success? Mostly by how we believe others perceive us, and how we perceive ourselves relative to others. The thought that we could be wrong, make a mistake or ask an embarrassing question is scary because we feel it would bring our competence into question. Making us lose in the race for perceived value.

We think that if we lack knowledge in front of someone in an equal or lower position, we will look stupid and inadequate. It will damage our reputation and authority. Maybe you can relate to this dialogue:

'My juniors won't respect me. They will stop following my instructions in the future. They will think I'm probably wrong again. What if they realize that there are more answers I don't have?'

Being wrong in front of the boss sucks. But that is a natural relationship because we are conditioned to accept it in the same way as the child/parent, and teacher/student relationships we looked at. But being wrong in front of subordinates? You may think you'll never be able to make another mistake again. Heaven forbid you are wrong in front of the boss and subordinates at the same time... Imagine those emotions.

So perhaps we only say and do things we believe will not damage how other people see us. If I do anything that threatens that image in my mind, then all the drama just described, plays out in the privacy of my mind. No one knows thank goodness. No one can hear my doubt and insecurity. They don't know that I don't understand some things. I am sure that it's only me that doesn't understand and everyone else does. I wish someone says something that helps me understand, or someone needs something explained.

Hell, the longer the time from when you were allowed to ask questions without looking like an idiot, the worse it gets. When you've been in a position for a long time, and there is anything you don't know, the threat of embarrassment is even greater.

That is a lot of weight to carry. If you can relate to any of that then take a few seconds to consider the following question.

How much energy does it take to deal with this every day?

I doubt most people think about this. How much energy it takes, how much it weighs? Stop for a moment and think about it. It is liberating to realize certain things. In this case, the tension we are placing on ourselves every day. The tension is real and so is the energy we use to cope with it without realizing that it's happening.

But the tension isn't necessary. It is the result of our percep-tions and assumptions. They are images we create to try and understand and predict the world around us. It is not something you have chosen. As we saw earlier, it gets programmed into us, and we let it continue 'just because'. We are imagining these terrible consequences based on nothing more than ideas.

We imagine the outcomes of the conversations we will have. We imagine what people will think and feel. But there is a difference between what we assume, and reality. It's like having a backpack we carry every day. In this backpack, we put the things we are dealing with. Until now, we haven't realized that we are carrying the fear of making mistakes and being wrong.

Do you accept that we use a lot of energy to manage the assump-tion that we need to know everything? Would you feel more free if we removed that internal tension?

If you can relate to what I've said, then you can see that I haven't told you something you didn't already know. Maybe you didn't think about it like that till now. Do you realize that most people around you, believe people will judge them for not knowing things too? Then doesn't it seem that most people are carrying that same tension? Is it possible that the people around you are holding back in the same way you are?

Some egos are so big that if an idea doesn't come from them, they can't handle it. If that's you, consider every little moment that has happened in your life up to this point. All the experience making you who you are. Surely every person around you has had their lifelong collection of experiences making them who they are. If you then believe that the person next to you has no value to add, regardless of who they are, then you are an ignorant, arrogant idiot. Don't be that guy...

If you are in a leadership position, then it's your responsibility to ensure that the best plan is formed using all the resources at your disposal. If you believe that all ideas must come from you, think about why you might be scared to let other people be valuable. When you find yourself thinking that you must be the center of attention for people to value you, remember that you are wrong. You are not worthless when you listen.

5

WORD POWER

How are you going to get through your next challenge? Are you going to accept that you don't have options? You have the power to change focus and commitment.

'Can you fix it?' seems like a pretty reasonable question. If the answer is no, then it's no, right? Well, that depends on how desperate you are. What happens when you can't afford it? You can't take no for an answer, and necessity becomes the mother of invention.

When you don't have money to feed your kids, or your child needs a heart transplant, but you have no money, do you give up? Would you accept no as an answer? You would find a way or make one. Then why give up easily on anything simpler, like changing a flat tire on a bicycle? Or building a website.

Notice how these sentences feel different.

Can you fix it?

vs

How are you going to fix it?

The second sentence already suggests that a solution exists.

Have you ever felt overwhelmed when something unexpected happens? It's natural to feel anxiety, stress, and defeat when something goes wrong. It is normal to feel uncertain, uncomfortable and intimidated when faced with new things.

Change your perspective. Use different words to encourage creativity. When you try this, you are going to be more creative, more effective, calmer, and in control.

6

THE COST OF DOING NOTHING

Who exactly is 'they'?

The farm grew fruit and veggies below the knee, nothing you needed a ladder to harvest. Work would start early to make the most of the cooler temperature. Everyone would sing and joke, taking special pleasure in the mornings because they would be in the sun until they went home. Even when they took a break they would need to sit in the sun since there were no trees. As the day wore on, they'd become tired and irritable. Every day while they rested, they would complain that there was no shade.

One day a new young girl named Helen came to work at the farm. During the lunch break, Helen heard the other workers complaining that there was no shade. She was new but she also thought it would be wonderful to have a tree to rest under at lunchtime. She asked one of the other workers why there were no trees. 'There should be, but the guys who were supposed to plant them never got around to it.' She asked why they didn't just do it themselves? 'Because we are too busy.'

Who is going to own it?

Can you see that the symptom (having no shade) is going to stay the symptom (still no bloody shade) until someone moves past the mental block and takes ownership? Are you willing to go to the boss and ask if you can take a couple of hours to solve this problem once and for all? Then plant a damn tree and go back to work. The solution will filter through as the tree grows.

Who is the 'they' that needs to do it? Who is taking ownership and responsibility? Who is going to get it done? Will you put your hand up and claim it? Maybe you need to convince the boss. Here are some ideas to help you. Will people have better rest in the shade? Will the boss get more work out of everyone after lunch if they had a better rest? What's in it for the boss?

Do the math.

The machine was down again. Sue's heart sank as she thought about breaking the news to the customer. Their extremely urgent job was going to be late. She felt someone else should make these calls, to feel what she has to go through every few days. 'Not again. Why can't the machines just stop breaking?' she says.

Customers send urgent work for the machine daily. But it breaks down every week or two. When the machine breaks down there is stress and pressure across their company, and their customers. There is also a risk to their reputation because they are late again. This has been going on for a while, at least 3 or 4 years.

It's a very old unit so the wires are all brittle. It's not a case of simply changing a fuse. It takes time to find the broken wire, so they lose a few hours each time it breaks. The machine needs it to be rewired, and they know it. To do that they'll need to stop it for a week.

The maintenance guy is always under pressure to fix it when it's down. He is frustrated because he wants to rewire the machine properly, eliminating electrical breakdown for the next 5 years. But there's pressure from everyone to get the current work out, so a quick fix plan is made each time. Find the broken old wire and join it. Just get it running to finish the job.

'We need the machine for these jobs then we'll stop it and fix it properly.' But it doesn't get shut down. As long as the machine is running there is no desire to shut it down. No one wants to tell customers that this machine is out of service for a week. Sometimes the finger gets pointed at the maintenance guy because it keeps breaking. Is he worth his salt? Someone needs the blame, right?

How many weeks per year is this machine broken down for? How much stress does it cost every single person involved? That includes the customer who doesn't know if he'll get his job on time. That is reputational risk, in other words, people don't trust you.

Is it inconvenient to take the machine out of service for a week? It's probably very uncomfortable. Would it be worth it to end this constant stress? Would this machine make more money if it keeps running, or keeps breaking?

7

FOCUS ON THE SOLUTION

Mark is in a stressful situation
Mark was furious when he got off the phone. His boss, Sandy, asked him what the problem was. 'I have a customer that is furious. She wants her to collect her order and it isn't here yet. Now she's shouting at me.'

Sandy asked if he had called the shipping company to find out how long it would be there. 'The guy from the shipping company was so rude. I called to ask for an update on the delivery but he was so unhelpful. He had such a horrible tone and told me it's on its way. My client is desperate for her stock and calls me every 10 minutes. I don't know what to tell her, she keeps shouting at me but I can't do anything more. She says we are useless and she doesn't know how we are still in business. I wish we could change to a different shipping company.'

Do you see what Mark is focusing on?
Mark is painting the scene. He is describing the emotional

experience. Spending nearly all of his words how on he feels. To convince Sandy that he is justified and she should be on his side, he must believe and act the part. Do you see how conveying those feelings will reinforce them? How much information does Sandy have to work with?

This is normal and it's ok to let Mark blow off some steam. But what if Mark's frustration is contagious and he infects Sandy? How often do you see it happen? Something happens to upset a friend or colleague, and we need to be upset with them. It's normal. But you know exactly what Sandy knows. Should she now get upset and start shouting at someone? What specifically does she know?

Mark has tried to show how unreasonable everybody is. Imagine Sandy stays calm and says she understands his frustration and that he needed to vent. Perhaps she now asks him to calmly tell her the facts so she can help him. Would that shift the focus back to finding a solution?

'A whirlwind does not last all morning.
A sudden shower does not last all day.
Who produces these things?
Heaven and earth!
Even heaven and earth cannot make wild things last long.
How then can people hope to do so?'

Tao Te Ching

8

QUESTIONS THAT WORK

Are you dealing with the symptom or the cause?

Recall the sailboat story with the cargo usually arriving late. Like everyone else, the manager is frustrated because the shipment is late. The fact that it's late is causing him stress, and he wants it to stop. Being late is not the cause of the problem, it is a symptom.

You may have noticed that in the story, there is a difference between what is possible and what is expected. 5 days of sailing is the best case if there is constant wind. But you can't control the wind. The loading and unloading also take extra time that wasn't accounted for.

Do you think it is reasonable to expect that the cargo is going to arrive in 5 days? Is it fair to say that they will continue to be disappointed? Will they continue to have irate customers?

Ask questions before you make a stupid statement.

It's easy to start by blaming someone when we are frustrated. It is also easy to make decisions immediately. Placing blame is such a normal response, that it seems natural. Here's something to start doing right now. Assume you are not seeing the true picture. That if you place blame, you'll be proven wrong and look like a fool.

In the long term, you need real solutions if you want to be effective and have less stress. By leading with good questions, we can gain the understanding we need.

So, what does a good question look like in this case?

They are fair and they don't judge. They are often very simple questions like asking someone to walk you through the process of what they do. The aim is to understand the other person's point of view. If you want to prove them wrong, then you should expect to fail. You miss the chance to find the cause of the problems. You will end up focusing on the symptom; in this case, being frustrated by late cargo.

Let's say you change the captain; do you think the problem will be solved? How frustrating will it be to try 10 different captains? Are they all going to be useless when the cargo is still late? Will the stress and frustration disappear?

You might be thinking this is obvious and I am wasting your time saying it. I think it's obvious too, but I still watch it happening every day. I hope you will start to see it too.

Questioning the standard

We already know that the expectation of 5 days is causing everybody involved a lot of stress. It is the benchmark time for the sailors, the office staff, and the customers. What is that standard based on? Whatever the standard is, does it make sense to the people that work with it?

Are you being lied to?

Here is an example I've seen several times. A machine stops because of an oil pressure alarm. Days are spent trying to fix the oil pressure problem with no success. The alarm remains. No one questions whether the information is false. The sensor sending the alarm is broken, the oil pressure is fine.

How much time do you have to make a decision?

No matter how urgent or scary something seems this is a great question. Whether you need cancer treatment or have a work dispute, figure out how much time you have to gather your thoughts.

Expensive is not a number.

When the word expensive is used, there is a good chance that the option won't be considered. Expensive is not a number, insist on a number. You'll be amazed how often this proves useful.

Being honest with yourself

Being honest with yourself is hard. Nothing defends you more than your own ego. It's the same for everyone. We make excuses for ourselves. Why is this important in a book about asking good questions? It comes back to assumptions.

If I am honest with myself as the captain in the story, then I can say that I didn't take the time to understand the people on land. What are the realities they deal with every day? The screaming clients, pressure from managers, and who knows what else. I assume they are taking my reality for granted, so I judge them to be idiots. They are unreasonable and they don't even try to see my side.

When I am asked by my friend if I told them to buy an engine, I said that I did. Was I lying? No. But am I being honest with myself? No. I was angry at his stupid question and defensive because I was being accused. I didn't ask the manager why he thought I was lazy. 'Could we go through the process and see if you can help me improve my decision-making?' 'Could we go through the information you are working with to see how it compares to mine?' Honestly, these questions didn't come up, both parties are frustrated and that's not going to change.

The boss is probably thinking 'I gave this guy a chance, but he is letting me down just like everyone else. We may have to shut down that part of the business if we can't move the cargo faster.' Do you really think your boss wants you to fail?

When last have you immersed yourself in the tasks you are asking people to do? Do you understand the challenges they face daily? Without judgment, not blaming anyone, just understanding. Accept that you have a right to your feelings, thoughts, and opinions just as they do. They know things you don't, everyone has value, even your enemy.

9

BUILD BRIDGES

<u>Getting on the same page</u>

When people disagree, they tend to take a position in support of their views, while taking a position against that of the other person. The position each of them holds becomes something to defend. I am right and you are wrong. How often have you seen it? Probably a few times a day at least. I'm sure you've seen one side saying that the other is stupid or something similar.

Let's first look at what doesn't work. You won't get a win/win if you start fighting with the other person. If someone says you are wrong, does it fill you with happiness? You probably want them to bugger off, even if you don't say so. If your child buys a car and you tell them it was a poor choice, do you think they are grateful for your comments? No, and you wouldn't be either if you had just bought the car. If you would shut down when hearing things like this, why would you think other people would be different?

You might believe you are right and prove the other person wrong. What will you achieve by hurting someone's ego? They won't thank you, they want you to bugger off. They may not like you or want to be your friend. They probably won't be trying to help you or work with you if they can avoid it. How important is it to you to break people down and prove them wrong? Do you want to be right, or do you want to be effective? Keep that golden rule in mind as we look at some ways to approach difficult situations.

Ann is a manager for a company that makes paper. Ben is a manager for a company that makes books. Both companies are owned by the same person. Charlie started the paper business because there wasn't enough paper in the country. Ann and Ben should be supporting one another but they aren't. Neither are achieving their daily targets and the boss isn't happy.

Charlie asks Ben why he hasn't made enough books. He blames Ann for not supplying the paper he needs. Charlie asks Ann why they are taking so long to deliver the paper. She blames Ben for asking her to squeeze in small orders which slows her down. Ann and Ben don't trust each other and don't get along. The situation has become difficult, they don't want to deal with each other. Charlie sends general manager Dan to sort it out, mostly because he doesn't want to look like the bad guy. Which is fair, he is paying people to manage after all.

Dan is no fool. He hears how people are blaming each other, but he has learned that things usually aren't what they seem. He doesn't want to threaten Ann and Ben to reach the target or get fired, he wants to help them achieve and exceed it. They have both been around for years and are good at what they do.

A lack of communication and understanding is usually the reason people struggle to resolve problems. If he doesn't take the time to understand the root problems, these two managers will think he is an idiot and won't trust or respect him. As it is, Ann and Ben aren't happy, and neither will take kindly to anyone blaming them. If Dan wants to be effective in helping them work together, he will have to earn their trust first. He visits each of them separately to prepare before getting them in one room.

Prepare

Step 1: Earning trust by listening and showing respect

The aim is to understand what they do and how they do it. Even if you don't like the person, they might still be the best person for the job. Even if you are sure you know what is happening, have the confidence to say nothing at this stage.

Why is it important that Dan only asks questions at the start? Firstly, they are both defensive because they are upset. He wants to calm things down by changing the focus from defending themselves, to teaching him. Secondly, he is probably going to learn things that will save him from looking like a fool.

If he asks Ann to teach him how they make paper, and what the challenges are, she won't need to defend herself. Dan gets to see Ann's point of view while picking up important details to help him understand. As they go through the process, he asks her questions about how a job moves from one workstation to another, and the challenges at each point. He asks what causes the most stress and what she would do differently if she could. Dan is truly interested.

At this first step, he doesn't want to change anything or make suggestions. When people shut down and the walls go up it's a bad time to correct them. It's time to understand and give people the opportunity to be heard. If you can't say it as a question, rather say nothing.

Be patient and mindful about the questions you ask. If your question implies that the person is wrong or stupid, then you are missing the point. Avoid arguing and let them talk. Everyone has value, even your enemy, so look for them.

If you have any observations think about how you share them. Understand that this person may not be wanting your advice outright. They may not even want you there. Only once the walls are down, and Ann has changed from a defensive mindset to an accepting one, will Dan test if it's safe to make a suggestion yet.

He doesn't make the suggestion directly. He asks Ann if she would be open to hearing an idea that might make her life easier. If her walls go back up and her tone becomes tense Dan will back off. He might add that he would love to get her thoughts on one or two ideas, but he'll wait. Ann may be very curious and open up at that which is great, if not that's fine.

When the suggestion is made, Dan asks it in the form of a question. He doesn't tell Ann what he thinks. He'll ask her why something is done the way it is now, then asks what she thinks about an idea he has.

Dan doesn't argue. This is still their space. If you want people to be open-minded then show you are open-minded. Don't expect other people to see things as you do. You may have planted a seed, now water it with acceptance. It's worth remembering that no one thinks they are part of the problem. You don't, I don't, so be patient.

This first step is the preparation phase. Dan does the same with Ben. Now he is going to get both sides together. What he wants is for each side to accept that he isn't out to get them. He wants them both to feel heard, understood and that he wants to help them succeed.

Getting them in a room

Speaking first

Speaking first allows him to direct their attention away from the tension between them. Dan wants to make sure that he doesn't give these two a chance to start fighting. He doesn't make statements or ask questions that make either of them defensive. Instead, he engages each of them separately and asks questions that highlight the challenges they face. The intention is to show Ben what the reality is for Ann and the other way around.

If Dan spent time with the two of them beforehand, he would have a much clearer idea of the situation they all face. He may have identified assumptions that are wrong. If he didn't meet with them beforehand, he would still go about drawing their attention towards understanding the situation instead of defending their positions.

Dan wants Ann to witness how he works to understand Ben's situation so that she can see things from his point of view. As they become aware of each other's needs, Dan hopes to have their help forming a plan to support each other. As you can see, Dan doesn't argue or accuse anyone at this early stage.

Dan realized that Ben was under a lot of pressure from Charlie not to turn away any order if there is no stock on hand. Charlie believes since he owns a paper factory, it is unacceptable to turn anyone away. A plan must always be made. Charlie expects Ann to continuously make different types of paper without losing time. Charlie often says he feels like he must do everything himself. There is always more to the story.

Letting others speak first

Dan learns a lot from watching people talk to one another. The words they use reveal much about what each person is thinking. He observes as much as he can about how Ann and Ben see each other. What matters to someone is not always said simply and clearly, so you can bet that their concerns aren't either. Listen to understand instead of listening to respond. What type of words, tones, and nonverbal body and facial expressions are they using?

He wants to help both sides, not pick sides. Staying neutral even if one is his friend and the other isn't. Are they working towards a solution or defending their positions? Are they making false assumptions about each other and the situation?

If they are using an aggressive or frustrate tone, Dan won't resist them. It's a golden opportunity to understand how they are feeling and why. He wants them to feel heard and get their frustrations out. This is not to say that he will let it get out of hand, he'll guide them to keep talking, asking questions to help him understand. If Dan doesn't give them room to release the emotion they are holding, it will still be there lowering their chance of success.

When you do speak

Dan is quick to admit that he doesn't know something and asks them to teach him. He is just as quick to admit what he has learned from both of them. If he suspects that Ben doesn't know something, Dan will say something like, 'Ann can I just make sure I understand this properly?' or, 'Ann would you mind explaining this to me again please?'.

In the chapter on understanding fear, we saw why Ben might want to avoid asking questions. Dan doesn't want to embarrass Ben. Instead, he'll show that it is safe to ask, that there is no judgment, by asking the question himself. But he needs to get the knowledge out in the open for everyone to be clear.

Dan isn't trying to be the man. He has seen time and again that if you want people to put their egos aside, even admit they are wrong, then you do it first. Show that there is no need to protect a status or position. The moment Dan humbles himself and admits he doesn't have all the answers, he lets go of the stress and weight of that expectation. Demonstrating to Ann and Ben that it's safe to do the same.

His only interests are the people and finding a solution with them. He doesn't go on a witch hunt to find out who is wrong or who is to blame. This is such a powerful thing to do that Dan does it in all areas of his life. He doesn't only use this technique to disarm resistance in a tough situation like this. It's how he relates with his family and friends, open, curious, and supportive.

Both sides are asked to help brainstorm a solution together with him. That allows for a plan that works for both and is most useful for the work to flow.

They all understand that they will need to involve Charlie. Both to manage his expectations and allow him to help them succeed. If they put together a clear image of how information and product currently flow, they may see where the confusion is. The solutions may be simple and possibly cost nothing. Even if there is a cost involved, they are all on the same page about how to support each other.

Moving forward

Everyone needs to be clear on the plan and what exactly their roles are. Dan doesn't want more than 3 key actions points before their next meeting. More action points make the focus unclear. Dan wants to keep things simple and clear, with everyone sure of what the most important tasks are. Everyone must be clear on what is expected of them for the follow-up meeting.

They may need to communicate at a specific time each day, including Dan and Charlie in the communication for the time being. There may be research that needs to happen on possible solutions. Maybe ask Charlie if he would be willing to help brainstorm a plan of action, with Ann and Ben, for them to run with.

Even if they identify 15 things that need attention, Dan will limit the action items before the next meeting to 3 or less. He won't add things like change toilet paper from 1 ply to 2 ply at this stage, because it makes the priority unclear. Whatever the actions are, they must be the most relevant. Everyone needs to be clear and accountable.

That last point is vital. The list will be kept small, but he won't accept either of them not doing their part on time. Dan knows that if he tolerates them not doing their part, then that becomes the acceptable standard.

Everyone involved is under additional stress because of this situation. If nothing changes, the stress and anxiety will continue. It doesn't only affect their work lives but personal lives as well. Dan is on a mission to change that. He wants to help people communicate better, getting everyone around a table, and talking honestly.

Dan isn't naive, he can't win over every person. There will be people who refuse to work with him, or anyone else trying to build a supportive team culture. He will have to take action against a person who insists on breaking down the team and morale. The whole team matters, and if one person continues to bring everyone down, then he will need to isolate that person. But he is a fair guy who believes that everyone has value, and needs to feel valued.

10

MENTAL JIU-JITSU TACTICS

<u>1: The bigger they are, the less they want to fall</u>

The room is full of industry heads. Three letter acronyms on their cards, usually starting with 'C' as in chief, like CEO, CFO, and COO, the need to protect status is strong in this room.

Danny has a deep understanding of mathematics and is giving a presentation to the chiefs who mostly hold degrees in accounting, business, and law. Danny is in charge of a model that all the chiefs are being forced to use in their organizations. They don't have a choice because the industry is asking for a government bailout.

One of the chiefs says they want the model to be running in three days and Danny insists that it will take two weeks. The main reason Danny is going to win is the confidence in her skill. It is very rare to find someone willing to challenge the technical person in this setting if they don't have the same level of understanding on the subject. Even though she doesn't have the status of anyone else in that room, the chiefs will not want to admit they don't understand, especially in front of their peers.

Thankfully Danny is ethical because none of the chiefs are prepared to be vulnerable which is dangerous if she isn't honest. As it is, everyone follows her lead because they are too scared to be wrong, even though they are the heads of various organizations.

Financial risk modeling is a very niche skillset, and there are very few people in the world who practice it. Is it reasonable that the chiefs would have experience in building complex financial models? Not really. But no one else in the room realizes that. Danny's confidence trumps the chief's desire to not look stupid.

2: When it's SIMPLE, don't say it's simple, show it...

Sam took up golf which is a notoriously difficult sport to start. After a time, his partner Alexis agrees to start so they can play together. She prefers to go for paid lessons and Sam respects that, and refrains for confusing the issue with more advice. He is just excited to have her join him.

Alexis still doesn't have a good golf swing and lacks confidence. With her coach going away for a while she needs to find a new coach. Sam has been watching and decides to seize the opportunity. He puts together a really simple way to think about the golf swing. He feels it's much simpler than what Alexis has been taught. He claims he can improve her swing with one bucket of balls. Alexis accepts the challenge.

Instead of thinking of the swing from the outside in i.e. the club, then the hands, then arms etc. it was more effective to start in the middle i.e. head, shoulders, and spine, and work outwards. Sam made it simple for Alexis and after practicing with just one bucket of balls, 'You're right, they focus on the wrong things.'

If you have found a way to make a complex issue simpler for yourself, don't expect others to know it can be easier just because you have figured it out, show them.

3) When it is COMPLICATED, don't say it's complicated, demonstrate it...

What happens when people think something is easy, and place unreasonable demands on you? Stress and tension build quickly because expectations won't be met. Earlier in our journey, you were sailing cargo across the sea. Those on land didn't realize how the wind affected your results. People seldom realize what work goes into a job well done. Here's an example of demonstrating complexity to gain respect and appreciation.

Danny's team found themselves in a difficult spot. They had made a system to perform regulatory financial models faster and cheaper. There aren't many people who can build those types of models. To help more people they built a system to automate some parts of the process.

Since Danny's team worked for a global audit firm, the audit partners were the people selling the service. This was great news for the team because the audit partners were well placed, had great relationships with their clients, and were highly effective salespeople. Work came in fast, too fast.

Danny's team couldn't keep up and there was a bigger problem brewing. The delivery times the partners were giving to their clients were impossible for this type of work. They promised their clients shorter times possible for audit work. That's a difficult situation because consulting businesses in the financial services space are very reliant on reputation.

These models typically take 3 to 6 weeks for a solid first version. If clients are being promised results in less than a week, you can imagine how quickly everyone goes from excited to furious. The partners can't honor their commitments to clients and the cost won't be accurate. You don't want to be the one to face that angry mob. Especially not if they don't think it should be a problem to get the work out in their usual time frames.

Danny's team takes the brilliant leadership initiative of putting together a presentation informing them of what timelines to expect. Danny is an incredibly talented person who understands these models in a way that few people in the world do. She has also become very good at communicating difficult concepts in simple ways.

After she puts the presentation together, she asks Steve to look at it. Steve has been around the team long enough to know how unique they are in what they do. And he knows that this beautifully simple presentation has a problem. It explains what the expected timelines are in a very clear and concise way. It doesn't explain why things take much longer than accounting and audit practices.

Firstly, each model is unique which takes much longer to build than standardized audit work. Secondly, in the audit field, you have many people trained in standard accounting and audit processes, with a fair amount of capable people joining the industry every year. If you need more people on a project in that field, you can add more people.

The same is not true for financial risk modeling. It is highly specialized with virtually no university training available at that time. The only way to learn was by doing the work, and you'd have to be exceptional at math. University courses only became available recently, and Danny helped make it happen. Unlike the accounting field, you can't simply add more people to a project because there aren't any.

Steve understood that the audience didn't have this perspective. While Danny's team worked for an audit firm, they did a very different type of work. They were more like engineers or scientists. This was where the big misunderstanding was happening, and Steve had an idea of how to help with that.

'You need to scare the crap out of them.' Steve said,' I know what you do and I'm telling that almost no one else does. The formulas you are using take up pages and most of it is literally in Greek. You need to make it real for them. Not to mention that the data you need is always an issue. When have you ever had data you could start using immediately?'

'Never.' Danny replied with a laugh.

Steve continued, 'You budget two weeks for that, but they don't understand why. It sounds like you are slow at fetching data which sounds like simply copying files to a hard drive. We both know that's not the case, but do you see how it sounds?'

'I do, so I'll explain how the process usually includes multiple client visits and time to clean it up' she said.

'Go further, don't just tell them, show them actual data sets that you use. Show them the programming that needs to happen too. I think they will have a new respect for what you do once they see it for themselves.'

Danny realized that what was normal for her and the team, was not normal for most people. She loved the idea and set about crafting a new presentation, sharing the reality of what makes the team so special. That presentation was a success. It achieved much more than just getting people to be more patient. It gained the respect and appreciation of the partners and opened more opportunities.

But why was it so impactful? Because she made it real for the audience. Don't say 'You don't understand' rather help them experience it for themselves.

4) Silence.
Ever noticed how awkward silence demands to be filled? If you can feel the pressure then you can bet the other person does too. Use it. Wait for the other person to fill it. Ask a question if you must, but sometimes you don't even need to do even that much. Then wait as long as it takes. Let the silence do the work. Don't be in a hurry, given time it's amazing how much information people will volunteer to stop the silence.

11

PEOPLE, PRODUCT, REWARD

There's such a simple and effective way to sell and influence people. I won't make bold claims about being the greatest salesperson alive, but I have sold millions across different industries. My bold claim is that it doesn't matter if it's a product, service, or idea. The same rules apply, and I have been successful because of them.

Obviously, you should learn how to generate and qualify leads. And you absolutely should learn to close properly. But there's a really simple reason why salespeople are blocked at the door, on the phone, and have their emails ignored. They don't give a damn about you. It's about their wants and needs. You have nothing to lose by trying this.

You might think you have to sound clever and know all the answers. Or that it's your duty to tell your customer all about your product and company and service and the features and the benefits and dazzle them with your enthusiasm. It's not about you. Take a genuine interest in them. Then you can use your sales knowledge to help them.

By all means, sell ice to an Eskimo if you feel it's a good way to build a relationship with him. Not sure how much he'll take or how loyal he'll be. Will he call to see if you've made target so he can help? Not a chance, Mrs. Eskimo will make him regret buying more ice long before that happens. You aren't putting the person ahead of your product.

True story 1 You have 10 minutes

A colleague and I were granted 10 minutes with the director of a company manufacturing truck trailers. My colleague was nervous because the client told him we'd be thrown out if we tried to sell him anything. My colleague kept saying nervously that this guy is 'hardcore'. I'd say, 'Relax bud, stop focusing on that, it doesn't matter.' He asked why I wasn't nervous. 'I would also be irritated if someone just walked in and tried to sell me something. I didn't come to sell him anything, I came here to make a friend.'

We didn't tell him about our company or products, we asked about his company. That meeting wasn't over in 10 minutes. He talked to us about what was important to him for more than an hour. In the end, he asked us what product we sold. He volunteered everything from that point. He also invited us to contact him if we ever wanted to sell for his company. That's right, he loved us, and we never talked about our business till we were asked. Put the person ahead of your product.

True story 2 What the hell do I know?

I was selling hardware to retail stores. I had recently joined the company and there was a store they hadn't sold to in six years. The store was given to me with the warning that the owner was difficult. My boss suggested I stick to new product ranges because this customer wouldn't take our tool range.

By all accounts, this guy was supposed to be impossible. He was also influential with other store owners. Imagine my boss's surprise calling me in under three months wanting to know how I had managed to get all our ranges into that store.

This guy's grandparents started the business, so he has been in hardware all his life. What the hell am I going to tell someone who has been a very successful operator, longer than I've been alive?

This is a man to be respected, with a wealth of knowledge. I asked him what advice he had for me to help the buyers at our company. I took notes and sent his suggestions through while I sat learning from him. He then placed orders without me asking. This man was respected by his peers but not by the people trying to sell to him. That seems crazy to me.

He had really good suggestions that come from a wealth of experience. He didn't think our buyers had made the best decisions. But because someone had finally asked for his help, he decided to support the brand. Put the person ahead of your product.

True story 3 Understanding what is important to someone

I was contracted to an engineering company. They were losing business in an outlying area. We weren't sure if business was slow or if the competition had been stealing our clients. When I went to meet those customers, I wanted to understand them, not sell to them. The truth wasn't obvious, and the customers involved were secretive.

One of the companies were sinking, trying desperately to keep its doors open. Cheap imported products were leaving these skilled employees jobless. It was a heartbreaking situation for me because the whole mining engineering industry is being crippled.

These companies make better quality products, but the imports are cheaper. In this case devastating countless homes, while a handful of people are making some quick cash. This isn't change for the better, it's irresponsible and selfish. We need innovation and disruption to help us.

His account with us had been placed on hold because he was struggling to pay. Talking with him it was apparent that he was now relying on one large order to save the business. He didn't want to say who it was and risk losing that last hope. But I was determined to help and did what I could to get better pricing on the material he would need.

At the other customer who had stopped ordering, I was impressed by the vehicles they were building. These guys weren't struggling, they were thriving. They were organized, and production was planned well in advance. They were proud that they didn't sacrifice quality by using cheap imports.

I wondered if perhaps this thriving company could help support my other customer in some way. It turned out this customer was already trying to support that first business. It was the big contract they were secretive about. This vehicle manufacturer had a reputation for manufacturing in-house which was important to them. But thankfully they were also passionate about damage to local engineering and were willing to act.

We were losing both customers because the one was on hold, and no one had picked up on it. Putting the people first allowed me to help them which led to the sales success. The vehicle manufacturer ended up buying the material for the contract from us on their account, further helping the engineering firm. People first, then product...

True story 4 From 400k to over 5 Million in two years

This was one account I was looking after while supplying cameras to retail stores. I was selling a premium brand and cost more than any of the others. The account I'm referring to has several photo printing stores. I'm highlighting this account because we sold more units in these stores than any other brand they carried. We were the most expensive and yet we outsold their own, equally famous budget brand. I made it my priority to make them feel supported. Helping them sell to their customers was more important than buying it from me.

At the same company, I had a customer in an outlying area. No other camera distributors were going out there. I was given this client because they had opened an account for a couple of purchases in the past. It was a mining and farming town miles away from anything. Taking the time to go out there turned out to be very profitable for both of us. It was a high-end audio store out in nowhere land. Wealthy miners and farmers had very few retail options, so this little store was doing surprisingly well. Because I took the time to care about them, they spent 100k a month with us going forward.

These were not isolated cases. They weren't even the biggest movers. Finding out what is important to other people matters. No matter what industry you're in. Here's my question to you. Do you feel important and valued when you are talking, or when you have to listen to someone? Most people want to be heard and acknowledged. Don't you think it's obvious that you will be more successful if you spend more time being interested in what other people have to say?

It's like this.
The world doesn't revolve around you. People will want you around if you make them feel good about themselves.

Don't argue, ask for advice.
You may be right and win the argument. But when you prove them wrong, you may hurt their ego and lose their support. There's the odd person here and there that you'll win over. And I'm sure it will stand out for you because it's something to brag about. But if you only knew how many more you've lost because of it. You will learn important things from listening instead. And you definitely won't hurt yourself, or your sales by trying

this.

Are you pushing a wheelbarrow or pulling a cart?

Putting the focus on yourself and your product is like pushing a wheelbarrow. It will work but you will limit yourself dramatically. Putting people first will be like using a horse and cart. If the horse comes first as it should, then you can move cartloads. When you see your next customer, are you going to be pushing a wheelbarrow?

12

MASTERING THE FIRST FEW SECONDS

Mat was angry and disappointed with himself. He had just been in a tense situation and as usual, didn't know what to say in the moment. Now that it was passed, he knew what he should have said. Going blank in the heat of the moment was frustrating. He didn't feel confident about being put on the spot because of it.

He thought of the funny things he could have said after the moment passed. Times he should have stood up for himself or someone else in a conflict situation but found himself at a loss. Job interviews or sales calls he had fumbled only to kick himself later. In the moment, he just couldn't think straight.

Mat had a friend named Steve. Steve went from being quick-tempered to being someone that people rely on to solve problems calmly in difficult situations. He decided to ask Steve what his secret was.

Steve said, 'I was frustrated with myself too. I used to read a lot of books on sales and negotiation, but I couldn't think straight when I was put on the spot. It was like I was blank and couldn't think of creative solutions when things became tense. My ideas would just vanish. Is that what you're talking about?'

'Yes, can you help fix it?'

Steve said, 'I have two tactics that I use together.'

Tactic 1: Know yourself

Step 1: Identify

Steve said, 'The first is understanding what is happening to your body. I started paying attention to what was happening to me in those situations. Road rage was one of the best times to observe myself.'

'Road rage? Are you serious?'

'Absolutely. It's very consistent if you think about it. The odds are good that you'll end up in situations while driving. When it does you can think about what you felt physically and emotionally.

I would get angry so quickly and go into a defensive mode. Physically I felt my blood rise and my hands would tremble. I was ready for a fight. I wasn't calm, and I wasn't in charge of my emotions. The chemicals my brain was releasing to handle conflict were stopping me from thinking clearly and creatively. The same thing was happening in other conflict situations like

59

dealing with difficult clients or being in trouble with the boss.'

Mat said, 'Ok that's interesting, I'll try it out but I don't like conflict. Do you still think this will work for me?'

'I don't think it makes a difference. If you tend to freeze up with fear, then that's what you should identify. In that case, remember this simple question, "Is someone trying to kill you with an ax?" if not, then what's the worst that can happen?

What matters is observing your first reactions in a stressful situation. What do you feel and what goes through your mind? We are all different, but I believe the first and most important thing is to know yourself first. Once you know what your body is doing, you've done the hardest part and you can move on to step two.'

Mat said, 'Ok that doesn't sound very hard actually.'

'You're right, what makes step one challenging is remembering to do it. When you're upset you might not remember to observe yourself until the moment has passed. It's important that you take that moment to focus on your body and mind as soon as you can.'

Step 2: Acknowledge

Steve said, 'Step two is recognizing that it's mostly chemicals and hormones making you react that way. Being aware of it means you know what's going on and you automatically start getting the power and control back.'

Mat said, 'Seriously? Just like that, I'll start thinking clearly in tense situations? Isn't there more to it?'

'Well, it is a process, but yes. Once you see it for what it is, it loses power. The more you become aware of it the more you master it.'

Step 3: Awareness

Steve said, 'Step three is simply shortening the time it takes you to recognize it. Once you recognize it in the moment, you have the power to control your emotions. Recognize when it's happening and accept it for what it is, some chemicals, then carry on in spite of it. When you do this, your body stops reacting badly to every little thing. Situations are just situations, not dramas.'

'Ok, I think I get it. It's like most things. It scares you until you understand it, then you become confident in your knowledge. Once you learn to ride a bike it seems easy.'

'Exactly. There's a saying about a clock losing its magic and mystery once you see how it works. Do you have any questions about the first tactic?'

Mat said, 'No, I'm ready for the second one.'

Tactic 2: Give yourself a moment

Steve said, 'This next tactic is powerful. There are so many ways to use this to your advantage. Give yourself a moment. There is no reason you can't tell people you are thinking. Why can't you? It's simple, "Please give me a moment.", "Just a sec, I'm thinking about it."'

Mat said, 'Wow, I never thought about it like that. It's funny actually.'

'Tell me if you've experienced this before. You get called into the boss's office, and the first thing going through your mind is, "Oh crap how much trouble am I in?" Or "What excuse can I use to shift the blame and avoid a warning?"'

'Oh, for sure.'

'Again, it's the uncertainty terrorizing you. You will be in a much better position to help yourself and the situation if you give yourself time to consider the facts. If you don't know the answer, simply say, "I need a moment to think about it." or, "I'm not sure, I need to go check."'

Mat said, 'But what if they demand an answer on the spot?'

'Fair enough, "I don't want to give you the wrong information. I'll be guessing, and I may be wrong. May I have time to get the right answers for you?" If it is something you should have known, "I am sorry, you are right, I should know this and I don't. May I find out and come back with the correct information? I will make sure I am on top of this in the future." Then make sure you are. If you made a mistake, own it. You gain respect if you do, you lose respect if you don't.'

Mat said, 'And by giving yourself time and slowing things down, you create time for the first tactic. You recognize your emotions and get control over them. That gives you the chance to think clearly, creatively, and find win/win solutions! Thanks Steve, I appreciate this. I can't believe I'm going to put road rage to good use.'

Steve said, 'No problem, I'm happy to help. Drive safe.'

Questions are these powerful tools that we take for granted, just like breathing. The act of breathing air is an essential part of life. We give it little to no thought until it's threatened. In just the same way that you can use a knife to save a life, you can use it to take a life.

Questions and genuine curiosity have the power to bring so much value to everything in your life. Once you start using it on purpose it's addictive. But there is a cost. The cost is willingness, the effort to be patient and consider other perspectives.

Your ego is an engine but being humble is your steering wheel. Sure, you can make a case for a bulldozing authoritarian approach, there's a time and place for it. There are times when, after careful consideration, you may decide to dramatically overreact. Losing your temper is a failure. Using your temper is a tactic.

This book is partly about emotional control and controlling your initiation reaction and temper. Control your temper, it is a tool just like your ego. Don't allow your temper or ego to be in charge. You don't need to be a slave to weak-minded tantrums. If you are, stop doing it, it makes you look like a fool.

People root for the underdog, so they'll want to see you fall. There is also a good chance you are looking foolish because you don't have the facts.

While you are at it, stop asking stupid questions, ask helpful ones instead.

Epilogue

'Therefore, cleaving asunder with the sword of wisdom the doubts of the heart, which thine own ignorance has engendered, follow the path of wisdom and arise!'

Bhagavad Gita

A place for your notes...

A PLACE FOR YOUR NOTES...

.

I hope something in here stays with you. Reviews will help this book get into the hands of someone who may find it helpful. That one simple act is an act of kindness to others.

Black Sheep

Black Sheep

About the Author

You can connect with me on:

🌐 https://www.savageinspiration.com
📘 https://fb.me/SavageBlackSheep

www.ingramcontent.com/pod-product-compliance
Lightning Source LLC
Chambersburg PA
CBHW071422040426
42445CB00012BA/1256